The Preparation Day, By C.s

the judgment hall, lest they should be defiled; but that they might eat the passover." Thus it would appear they returned to finish the passover by eating the lamb at the very hour they delivered Jesus to the Gentile power to be tried and killed. (John xviii. 28.)

If we turn now to John xix. 14 we shall find a still more blessed explanation: one full of the deepest instruction for our *hearts*. You will notice it is not the preparation *for* the passover, but *of* the passover. And even after the crucifixion we read, "And now when the even was come, because it was *the preparation*, that is, the day before the sabbath." (Mark xv. 42.) "For that sabbath day was an high day." (John xix. 31.) That is, the sabbath of the passover week was of all sabbaths the highest type of eternal rest. For fifteen centuries *the preparation* day had pointed on to this day, on which let us now dwell. Jesus, the Lamb of God, had presented Himself at this very passover, when *the passover day* fell on the day before the sabbath. Alas! the Jews understood it not. Do they who say they are Jews understand it any more now?

The preparation day, then, commenced on the Thursday evening at sunset, and lasted until Friday evening sunset. But what was it the preparation for? It was God's preparation day for man, poor, lost, guilty man, to be brought into eternal rest to Himself: the eternal sabbath based on redemption. This had long been fore-shadowed in Deuteronomy v. 15: "And remember that thou wast a servant in the land of Egypt, and that the Lord thy God brought thee out thence, through a mighty hand, and by a stretched-out arm: THEREFORE the Lord thy God commanded thee to keep the sabbath day." The sabbath, or rest of creation, had long been lost, and now God set forth the sabbath of re-demption, which never can be lost whilst God is faithful to the claims of the redemption-blood of His Lamb.

Oh that our eyes may be fastened on Him, the Lamb of God, during the twenty-four hours of this preparation day. In this year the passover day was the preparation day. When the hour was come at the beginning of this day (6 p.m. of our Thursday) He sat down. Let us hear His precious words. "With desire I have desired to eat this passover with you before I suffer. For I say unto you, I will not any more eat thereof, until it be fulfilled in the kingdom of God." (Luke xxii. 15, 16.) Think what He had to endure that day to fulfil the passover, and prepare the sure ground of our eternal rest. Yet such was His love to us, He could say, "With desire I have desired to eat this passover with you before *I suffer*." Thus began the preparation day. There was no more use for the thousands of dying lambs. No more use for their flesh, nor typical value in their blood. The material feast must cease, and the spiritual nowbe symbolised by the bread and wine. The Lamb of God presents Himself. "And he took bread, and gave thanks, and brake it, and gave unto them, saying, This is my body, which is given for you: this do in remembrance of me. Likewise also the cup after supper, saying, This cup is the new testament in my blood, which is shed for you." The blessed Lord well knew the way these words would be perverted to a literal meaning of His flesh and blood, and thus He uses a word to shew it was not literal: He does not say which shall be, but which *is*. Indeed, another word also: "This cup." Now the blood was not yet shed, and the *cup* was not His blood. Did He not clearly mean, that as the paschal lamb had been eaten by Israel, in *remembrance* of the temporal redemption from Egypt, so it is His blessed will that we should partake of the symbols of bread and wine in remembrance of Him and of our eternal redemption? Nay, He says, "Do this in remembrance of me." We shall find He finished the work of this preparation day, and left no need of another sacrifice to bring men into the sabbath of eternal rest.

Let us return to John for further details of the preparation day. Chapter xiii. Supper, the passover supper, being come, there was Judas, the devil having put into his heart to betray Him; but Jesus knew His own, and loved them with a love that knows no end. "He riseth from supper, and laid aside his garments." This was probably at the usual break in the passover, before the lamb was eaten, when the head of the household catechised the younger children in the word. Did not the washing of their feet by water signify how He would ever, in love, apply the word? What a precious lesson on the preparation day! He will ever keep us suited to the rest into which we are brought. And thus He would have us serve each other.

He may have felt the first pang of suffering as He washed the feet of Judas; for when He had sat down again we read, He was troubled in spirit, and testified and said, " Verily, verily, I say unto you, that one of you shall betray me." This produced great consternation. And well it might. And what a remembrance for Judas for ever and ever! And what does the tender heart of Jesus still feel as He sees men reading the word, and enjoying every outward privilege of Christendom, and yet hastening on to where Judas went? It will be terrible in hell to remember a father's prayers and the constant reading of the word; and a sister or a brother resting in the love of Jesus, as one disciple leaned on Jesus' bosom. Well may we look round the family, and ask, Lord, who is it? Are you quite certain, reader of these lines, the doom of Judas will never be yours? Oh, what did the blessed Jesus feel when He dipped the sop and gave it to Judas? It was all over for that man. Satan entered into him, he went out, "and it was night." And a night to his soul that will *never*, *never* know the break of day. No hope. What a warning on the preparation day!

And the bold and devoted Peter must learn this day, that he has *no strength*. It is not what Peter can do for the Lord on the preparation day, it must be the work of the Lord for him.

And it was on this preparation day that the veil was lifted up, and the heavenly place and home of the saints fully revealed for the first time. (John xiv. 1–3.) Jesus would be no longer the object of sight; but the object of faith, even as God. These poor disciples are lifted up, far above the promises to Israel, up to the Father's house with its many mansions. He says, "I go to prepare a place for you, and if I go and prepare a place for you, I will come again and receive you unto myself; that where I am, there ye may be also." Is not all this revelation suited to be given on preparation day? If on that day He would do the work that redeems us and prepares us for the place on high, then it was the fit time to tell them and us that He would go and prepare the place, and come and take us to Himself.

But if a Peter has no strength in the hour of temptation to stand for Christ, and Christ is no longer with us in bodily presence to sustain us, what is to become of us until He comes? He says, on this preparation day, "I will pray the Father, and he shall give you another Comforter [one to take entire charge of you], that he may abide with you for ever, even the Spirit of truth." See how this is repeated so as to meet our need in every way. (John xiv. 16, 18, 26; xv. 26; xvi. 7–14.) Nay, all the blessed instruction of John xiii., xiv., xv., xvi. And then the claims of Christ for us in chapter xvii. All this occupied after supper the evening of preparation day, and every word is needed for our souls. The great work, however, of the preparation day had not yet begun. Let us carefully notice each stage. The preparation day had advanced. "When Jesus had spoken these words, he went forth with his disciples over the brook Cedron, where was a garden, into the which he entered, and his disciples." Let us go with Him into the garden, and witness the sorrows of our own dear Lord.

As Jesus crossed the Cedron and entered the garden of Gethsemane for the last time, in the dark night of that preparation day, no human heart could sympathise with Him. No, to all His disciples it was the day of deepest disappointment. None knew the Father but the Son. None knew what was in the heart of God our

Father but He. God is love, and God had sent
His Son that man might be brought into the
eternal sabbath of rest. This was the purpose of
God; and this was the preparation day, fore-
ordained from all eternity, in which that work
should be accomplished; yes, finished that very
day. A work that should rend the veil, and re-
move every obstacle, should open the way for
you and me and every guilty sinner that believes
God into His own eternal rest—a sabbath that
can never be broken—eternal rest based entirely
on the work accomplished on that preparation
day.

Never was there a day like this before; never
can there be another like it throughout the ages
of eternity. Every promise, and every sacrifice;
yea, all the dealings of God with man had refer-
ence to this preparation day. All this was
known to Jesus. And when they had sung a
psalm they went out and went into the Mount of
Olives. Now what was it that pressed upon the
heart of Jesus? What was there so terrible
before His soul? He said unto them, "All ye
shall be offended because of me this night: for it
is written, I will smite the shepherd, and the
sheep of the flock shall be scattered abroad."
(Matt. xxvi. 31.) It was not merely what He
was about to endure in all the mocking, and cruel
torment, that men could inflict; but, as the shepherd, though equal with God—His fellow, yet He

must be smitten by Jehovah. Oh, think of the holy, holy, holy Son being made a curse beneath the smiting of Jehovah. Must this be accomplished on the preparation day? He would need and would look for sympathy, but all would forsake Him. And all to bring us into rest. How tenderly He said, "Sit ye here, while I go and pray yonder." Oh, look at Him there, "And being in an agony, he prayed more earnestly; and his sweat was as it were great drops of blood falling to the ground." What a cry that the cup might pass from Him! And what subjection to the Father's will. The Lamb must be killed. He gave Himself up.

None but the Father knew how He loved the church, when He thus gave Himself up for it. Deep was the sorrow and anguish of His heart when He took with Him Peter and the two sons of Zebedee. Hear Him: "My soul is exceeding sorrowful, even unto death: tarry ye here, and watch with me." In Matthew it is, when He had gone a little way from them, He "fell on his face, and prayed, saying, O my Father, if it be possible, let this cup pass from me! nevertheless, not as I will, but as thou wilt." In Mark, He said: "Abba, Father." My Father, Abba Father. He appeals to all the endearing affection of that eternal relationship. But He could not be heard. He said: "Our fathers trusted in thee; they trusted, and thou didst deliver them. They cried unto thee, and were delivered; they trusted in thee, and were not confounded. But I am a worm, and no man: a reproach of men, and despised of the people." (Ps. xxii. 4-6.) Oh, the depths into which our precious holy Jesus sank on that preparation day! But there was no other way by which the guilty sinner could be brought into the sabbath of God.

And what was the sympathy of His chosen three? He found them asleep, for their eyes were heavy. But nothing changed His change-less love. Three times did He thus go and cry to the Father, His Father. Three times did He return to find His most devoted disciples asleep. Yes, such is even devotedness, when put to the test. And if such is devotedness, what is mere profession?

A little noise is heard in the garden. The dreadful cup must be drunk: Here comes a very apostle of profession, at the head of a band of men, with swords, and staves, from the religious authorities of Israel. Hear what he says: "Now he that betrayed him gave them a sign, saying, Whomsoever I shall kiss, that same is he; hold him fast. And forthwith he came to Jesus, and said, Hail, Master; and kissed him," or covered Him with kisses. Such is man, whether it be a devoted disciple, or a false apostle. Jesus, blessed Jesus, thou must do the whole work alone on that preparation day!

In John, at this trying hour, the Godhead shone out for a moment: as "Jesus said unto them, *I am* he, they went backward and fell to the ground." And now the last act of Jesus before He was bound was to heal His enemy's ear. Peter could sleep when he ought to have been watching, and he would fight when the hour had arrived to be yielding. But Jesus was perfect in His deepest humiliation. He who had made all things gives Himself up to be bound.

We now enter on another stage of sufferings of Jesus on the preparation day. He is bound by His own people, and they take Him, the holy, holy One, as a criminal. They led Him first to Annas, father-in-law to Caiaphas the high priest. We have not much account of what He suffered before him. We read that he sent Him bound unto Caiaphas, the high priest. (John xviii. 13–24.)

Now mark the sufferings of Jesus, God manifest in the flesh, before His own high priest. What He suffered at his hands was as the Captain of our salvation. Just an example of what His followers have ever had to suffer if the pretended priesthood have had the power, whatever the name by which that priesthood was known. Surely no just charge could be made against the pure and spotless One. And the priest tried to entangle Him in His words. "Jesus answered him, I spake openly to the world; I ever taught in the synagogue, and in the temple, whither the

Jews always resort; and in secret have I said nothing. Why askest thou me? ask them which heard me, what I have said unto them," &c. (John xviii. 19–21.)

What a revelation of man: "Now the chief priests and elders, and all the council sought false witness against Jesus to put him to death." (Matt. xxvi. 59.) How often have the priests of Rome, pagan and papal, done the same thing. What parallels we might give from the history of God's real saints. Mark, the sole object of the Jewish sanhedrim was the death of the Holy One, Jesus.

No false witnesses could be found to agree. Driven to the last extremity, the high priest adjures Him by the living God, that He should tell them whether He was the Christ the Son of God. How blessed the answer of Him who is the truth. "Jesus saith unto him, Thou hast said: nevertheless I say unto you, Hereafter shall ye see the Son of man sitting on the right hand of power, and coming in the clouds of heaven." The high priest ought to have known that the Messiah would come exactly in this manner, as may be seen in Daniel vii. 9–14; Micah v. 1–3. The word of God was perfectly clear, and the Christ of God stood before him; but he knew it not. All was blasphemy to the high priest. And what was the thought of chief priests, elders, and sanhedrim? "They answered and said, He is guilty of death."

(Matt. xxvi. 66.) All that He had said was the exact truth. Man has no heart for the truth.

Mark well how religious man treated the Lord of glory. "Then did they spit in his face, and buffeted him; and others smote him with the palms of their hands (or with rods)." This gave much torment and extreme suffering. Ah, what would be said in our day if a highwayman was treated as they treated the Holy Son of God, against whom no charge of sin could be brought?

We read further in Luke xxii. that "the men that held Jesus mocked him and smote him. And when they had blindfolded him, they struck him on the face, and asked him, saying, Prophesy, who is it that smote thee?" And in the midst of all this unparalleled outrage and inhuman cruelty, and anguish, and suffering, was there no human heart to pity or sympathise? No; as we read in Psalm cxlii. 4, "I looked on my right hand, and beheld, but there was no man that would know me; refuge failed me; no man cared for my soul." But what of Peter, who really in his heart loved Jesus; Peter, who sincerely thought and said he would die for Jesus? What was he doing when Jesus was blindfolded and cruelly smitten by brutal Jews? Hush, whilst we tell it; he was denying Jesus, with cursing and swearing. Can we desire a greater proof that we cannot trust in ourselves, or our love, or our promises? We have now seen in this first trial of Jesus, what the man under law is with all his privileges. The Jew stands thus before us on the preparation day; he had every possible privilege; the oracles of God and His prophets had foretold these sufferings of the Messiah. Never in the history of the Jew had he made greater professions of zeal for the religion of his fathers. The law commanded him to love God with all his heart. And now God incarnate, visible in humanity, humbled, in love to man, love to them : Jesus was delivered up into his hands. And the full character of the most favoured man was fully revealed. What is in man came out in all its envy, malice, and hatred, against the Son of God. The chief priests seem to have been the worst. How strange, the greater the pretensions, and the more highly esteemed amongst men, the greater the wickedness and hatred to God.

Thus the midnight hours of the preparation day passed on. Deeper sorrows yet awaited our adorable Lord. Let us trace them ; for all hearts must be tested on this preparation day. The whole multitude now arise and lead Him bound, again to tramp the dark streets of Jerusalem. They are taking him to Pilate. They are determined He shall be given up to the Gentile power. . They long that He shall die the most cruel and shameful death. Let us follow, and see if the Gentile is better than the Jew.

It is now approaching morning on the preparation day. Remember how Jesus had been beaten, spit upon, and mocked at His trial before the high priest. "And straightway in the morning the chief priests held a consultation with the elders and scribes and the whole council, and bound Jesus, and *carried him away*, and delivered him to Pilate." (Mark xv. 1.) The Jews could convict Him of no sin, and Pilate can find *no fault in Him.* He fully declares this. He is greatly puzzled. He knows well that for envy the Jews had delivered Him to him.

Oh, what a sight! The weary, bruised, beaten Jesus! There He stands: see how His blessed face has been smitten. And there stand the multitude of the Jews, fiercely accusing the Prisoner, who created the universe. Yes, the whole multitude of them arose and led Him to Pilate. And in their cruel hatred they could only belch out lies against the Holy One. "We found this fellow perverting the nation, and forbidding to give tribute to Cæsar," &c. And when the Roman governor declared he could find no fault in Him, they were the more fierce.

Pilate, hearing He was from Galilee, seeks to escape from his difficulty by sending Him to Herod, who happened to be in Jerusalem at this time. Yes, every possible insult must be heaped upon the Lamb of God. He must be led again through the dark streets of Jerusalem to stand

before the wicked Idumean Herod—the volup-
tuous, cruel murderer.   And this wicked man
was glad, and hoped to have his curiosity
gratified.   Not a single word of complaint, even
now, escapes the holy lips of Jesus.   " He
answered him nothing."   Blessed Jesus, may we
learn of Thee !

And the chief priests and scribes stood and
vehemently accused Him.   They followed Him
like bloodhounds on this preparation day.   Yes,
they accused Him, their Messiah, to the murderer
Herod.   They had blindfolded Him, and beaten
Him with rods, and in the face.   And is there
any pity in the heart of Herod ?   Just as much
as the true followers of Jesus have found,
and may again find, in the dungeons of the
Inquisition.   " Herod with his men of war set
him at nought, and mocked him, and arrayed him
in a gorgeous robe, and sent him again to Pilate."

Thus, O Jerusalem, was thy Jehovah, King,
and Lord, dragged and mocked by the cruel
crowd through thy dark streets.   Not a word of
pity, or a look of sympathy for Him, who came
to do the Father's will.

Pilate felt the deep wickedness of the chief
priests and rulers of the people.   Again he tries
to set Him free.   He says, " I, having examined
him before you, have found no fault in this
man touching those things whereof ye accuse
him." (Luke xxiii.)   Herod, too, had pronounced

no sentence of death on Him. The struggle to
release Him was made still greater by a message
from his wife. This poor Gentile alone pleads
for Jesus with Pilate her husband. She says:
" Have thou nothing to do with that just man;
for I have suffered many things this day in a
dream because of him." (Matt. xxii. 19.)

Pilate tried hard to escape the evident guilt of
giving up " that just man " by using his privilege of releasing one prisoner at the feast of
passover. But no, the Lamb must die on this
passover day. The chief priests demand His
death, and deliberately prefer a murderer and a
robber to the holy and the just One of God—the
Lamb without spot. They demand that Jesus
shall be crucified. And now Pilate joins them
in their wickedness. No evil could they lay to
His charge, " But they cried out the more, saying,
Let him be crucified. When Pilate saw that he
could prevail nothing, but that rather a tumult
was made, he took water, and washed his hands
before the multitude, saying, I am innocent of
the blood of this just person ; see ye to it." Then
the bold words from the Jews were uttered:
" His blood be on us, and on our children."

And what did this representative of the
Gentile power then do, convinced, judge as he
was, that there was no fault in Jesus? He
deliberately released the robber and murderer.
And then what? Was there a little respite now ?

Was the bruised and beaten prisoner, the declared just One, allowed to rest His weary body awhile? The first thing done was to inflict the cruel torment of the Roman lash—a torment under which prisoners often died. Pilate has Him stripped and scourged. How that back was torn with the cruel lash!

Isaiah, more than 600 years before, had described this scene. He who clothes the heavens said, "I was not rebellious, neither turned away back: I gave my back to the smiters, and my cheeks to them that plucked off the hair; I hid not my face from shame and spitting." (Is. l. 6.) "He was oppressed, and he was afflicted, yet he opened not his mouth: he is brought as a lamb to the slaughter, and as a sheep before her shearers is dumb, so he openeth not his mouth." (Is. liii. 7.) Yes, He loved the church and gave Himself for it. Oh, look at that bleeding, bruised Lamb of God, silently suffering all the cruel agony that man could inflict!

How long they tare His back we are not told. Surely this was enough! No. He was now given up to the brutal Roman soldiers. The whole Gentile band was called together. And after all that He had suffered at the hands of His own people the Jews, was there no pity, no relaxation in the cruel torture? No, none! The first twelve hours of the preparation day had about closed (John xix. 14) and the first of the

measured three hours began with the scourging,
about the sixth hour of Roman time: and lasted
until the third hour of Jewish time (9 A.M.)
when He was crucified.

What took place during these three hours?
The awful scourging. This may have been
nearly unto death. But all was borne in holy
silence, the silence of undying love. No tender
hand to wash and dress those bleeding wounds.
They took Jesus after the awful torture into the
common hall. Patiently He bore the pain as
they stripped Him there, "and put on him a
scarlet robe. And when they had platted a
crown of thorns, they put it on his head, and a
reed in his right hand. And they bowed the
knee before him, and mocked him saying, Hail,
king of the Jews!" Oh, hold! is not this
enough? No, no. "And they spit upon him,
and took the reed and smote him on the head."
And when they, the Gentiles, had had their fill of
cruel torture and mockery, then Pilate must add
one more act of deep degradation. At this very
time when the soldiers were wearied out with
their mockery, and beating Him with their
hands; whilst Jesus was wearing the crown of
thorns and the purple robe, "Pilate therefore
went forth again, and saith unto them, Behold, I
bring him forth to you, that ye may know that I
find no fault in him. Then came Jesus forth,
wearing the crown of thorns and the purple

robe. And Pilate saith unto them, BEHOLD THE MAN!"

Behold the man! Ah, behold the Lamb of God! See the blood drop from His holy crowned brow! Yet this is He who shall come in glory and shew that nation his wounded hands. And is there no melting of the Jewish hearts to Him? Was ever sorrow like His sorrow? No, the very priests cried out again, "Crucify him! Crucify him!" Pilate at last delivers Him up to them.

There was no rest for Jesus on the preparation day. The soldiers spit on Him, and smite Him on the head, and then take the robe from off Him, and put His own raiment on Him, and led Him away to crucify Him. Oh, what He went through during these three hours from His condemnation to the cross! His perfectly tender human heart needed sympathy; but lover and. friend were far from Him.

It was customary to compel the malefactor to bear his own cross to the place of execution. From John we learn this was carried out on Jesus. After all the beating, scourging, smiting on the head, and torture, we read, "And he bearing his cross went forth." (John xix. 17.) In Luke xxiii. we read, "And as they led him away, they laid hold upon one Simon, a Cyrenian, coming out of the country, and on him they laid the cross, that he might bear it after Jesus." Was this pity to Him in His extreme weakness?

No, from all we have seen they may have feared He would die on the way, and so they might lose the Satanic gratification of witnessing His torture on the cross.

Oh, look at that last procession on the preparation day. All that was past was as nothing to what was before Him, yet to come. He was about to drink the dreadful cup of wrath due to millions of souls. Let us look at the procession in Luke xxiii. 27. It is now approaching nine o'clock A.M. A great company of people follow Him. "And of women, which also bewailed and lamented him. But Jesus turning unto them said, Daughters of Jerusalem, weep not for me, but weep for yourselves, and for your children." His tender heart was occupied with the terrible judgments so soon to fall on them and their city. What love! God is love.

One other indignity must be added, that the words of Isaiah might be fulfilled, "And he was numbered with the transgressors." (Is. liii. 12.) "And there were also two other malefactors, led with him to be put to death." What a sight! He who was God, walking with two thieves, to that place where the great work of the preparation day must be accomplished, that shall bring lost sinners into the sabbath, the rest of God. The procession halts at a place of a skull, Calvary. "There they crucified him, and the malefactors, one on the right hand and the other on the left." This is at the third hour of Jewish time, or 9 o'clock A.M. The cross was not merely an instrument of death, but of *torture* and death, the most prolonged and painful torture. The six hours' torture are divided into two distinct parts. Let us inquire what took place in each.

We have traced the holy sufferer through the hours of the preparation day until the third hour, or nine o'clock A.M. In His last journey He halted at the place of crucifixion. We read the words, but how little can we realise the depth of degradation to the holy, holy Son of God. Let us meditate on what took place during the first three hours on the cross, until twelve at noon. What is crucifixion? At first it was an instrument of death, shameful and cruel. The poor criminal was stripped naked, a sharp stake was placed in the ground with the point upwards. This was driven through the body of the living prisoner, upwards to the heart, and there he was impaled to die! But this was a merciful death compared to the mode used in the days of our Lord.

A hole was dug in the ground to receive the beam of wood. The feet were nailed to that wood and the body laid in awful agony on the same, and the hands nailed to the cross part at the top. Then think of the torture of the body as the cross was lifted up, and let fall in the hole prepared. It was at this supreme moment of

untold pain that Jesus said, "Father, forgive
them, for they know not what they do." For
three hours He hung there on that shameful
cross, brutal soldiers mocking Him, rulers derid-
ing Him. Oh, behold Him there crucified between
two thieves. "And the scripture was fulfilled
which saith, And he was numbered with the
transgressors." And there the unfeeling crowd
pass by, wagging their heads, and saying, "Ah
thou that destroyest the temple, and buildest it
in three days, save thyself, and come down from
the cross." The priest, yes, the chief of them,
joined in the mockery. The very thieves reviled
Him. (Mark xv. 25–32.) Oh, for three hours
they sat down and watched Him endure the
torture of the cross.

But what was the inward experience of our
adorable Lord, as He hung there in cruel suffering? He tells how the fathers had trusted in
God, and were delivered, "But I am a worm, and
no man . . . and despised of the people. All they
that see me laugh me to scorn: they shoot out
the lip, they shake the head, saying, He trusted
on the Lord, that he would deliver him: let him
deliver him seeing he delighted in him." Oh,
read the unheard sighs of Jesus in Psalm xxii.
Was ever sorrow like His sorrow? In the midst
of all the cruel mockery, only one voice was
heard that owned Him Saviour, Lord. One of
the reviling thieves was given to Him, as He

hung there on the cross. He had heard those gracious words, " Father, forgive them ; for they know not what they do." Faith was given to the dying thief: precious grace. May we not also still pray, Father, forgive the living thieves all around in this day, who are robbing Jesus of His glory as the Saviour of sinners, and the giver of eternal life, yea, denying His divinity and atonement for sins—for they know not what they do ? But oh, wretched men, beware lest your doom be not that of the dying thief, but that of Judas. For surely the man that pretends to be a minister of Christ, and is a betrayer of the scriptures into the hands of the infidels, is more like Judas than like the dying thief.

Oh, how full the answer of Thy heart, blessed Jesus, to the faith of the tortured dying thief : "Verily, I say unto thee, To-day shalt thou be with me in paradise." Yes, he was justly put out of this sinful world, but in grace he was to be with Thee in the paradise of God.

It would appear to have been about noon when Jesus thus spoke to the converted thief, the sixth hour of Jewish time. (Luke xxiii. 43, 44.) "And when the sixth hour was come, there was dark-ness over the whole land until the ninth hour." (Mark xv. 33.)

And why is there so little said in the Gospels as to what the holy, holy Lord suffered during those three last hours ? Surely it is because it

cannot be told. It can only be known to God
what Jesus then suffered for us, for our redemption. We only hear the final bitter cry, "My
God, my God, why hast thou forsaken me?"
Darkness covered Him from every eye but the
eye of God. Oh, think of Him being made sin
for us; of all God's billows rolling over His soul;
of all our sins, dear fellow believer, laid on Him
—delivered for our offences, bearing our iniquities
—the infinite wrath of God, which could only be
borne by the infinite One.

And now He cries, with a loud voice, "It is
Finished, and he bowed his head and gave up
the ghost." (John xix. 30.) Nothing now re-
mained, but to take down the precious body and
lay it in the sepulchre. The great work of the
preparation day is finished. Every scripture is
fulfilled; all the shadows of the law pass away.
The one atoning sacrifice has been offered. Will
God accept it? What was the preparation for?
The sabbath of the passover week, the sabbath
or rest of redemption. As we have seen, God
gave the sabbath to Israel because they were
redeemed, as a shadow of this rest, or sabbath, to
come. Well, let us see what took place. The
body of Jesus is laid in the sepulchre at the close
of the preparation day. The great stone was
laid on the mouth of the sepulchre.

Did God raise Him from the dead on the
Jewish sabbath, and thus restore man to rest

under the sabbath of the law? No; Jesus lay in the sepulchre all through the sabbath given to Israel. The eternal sabbath of rest for man must be entirely new—the rest of the new creation. We cannot express in words how entirely all was changed, and all the effect of the work accomplished on the preparation day. When that work was finished the veil was rent. The way of approach to God was opened—opened also was the way for God to come out to man in richest, fullest grace. But this must be by first raising Jesus from the dead. He must be the first-fruits of them that slept. If He be not risen, all He suffered was in vain, as is fully shewn in 1 Corinthians xv. "But now is Christ risen from the dead, and become the first-fruits of them that slept." Oh, what a first day of the week was that, when God raised Christ from the dead! Could He have given a greater proof that He accepted the work done on the preparation day? The grave clothes were laid peacefully aside, "and the napkin, that was about his head, not lying with the linen clothes, but wrapped together in a place by itself." How little the disciples understood what had been accomplished on that preparation day! "For as yet they knew not the scripture, that he must rise again from the dead."

What were the first words Jesus spoke to His disciples when He was risen from the dead?

" Peace be unto you.   And when he had so said.
he shewed unto them his hands and his side.
Then were the disciples glad when they saw the
Lord." Yes, He had made peace by His own
blood on the preparation day. He shewed them
His hands and His side. The work was done. It
is finished. They heard Him speak unto them.
We also are assured by the inspired word that
righteousness is reckoned unto us, " if we believe
on him that raised up Jesus our Lord from the
dead; who was delivered for our offences, and
was raised again for our justification. Therefore
being justified by faith we have peace with God,
through our Lord Jesus Christ, by whom also we
have access by faith into this grace wherein
we stand, and rejoice in the hope of the glory of
God." (Rom. iv. 24, 25 ; v. 1, 2.)

What a sabbath of rest, entirely through the
work accomplished on the preparation day !
Now, if you saw Jesus, if He appeared to you,
and you looked at His wounded side and wounded
hands, and He were to speak to you with His
voice, " Peace unto you," just as He did to His
disciples, would not that make you perfectly
happy? Well, He says, " Blessed are they that
have not seen, and yet have believed." Do you
believe He died for your sins according to the
scriptures ? Do you believe that God raised Him
from the dead for the purpose of your justification ? And believing this, do you know that you

Ingram Content Group UK Ltd.
Milton Keynes UK
UKHW020106090323
418239UK00006B/561